The Sacred Archetypal Code

Dr. Edward Schellhammer

The Sacred Archetypal Code. 1st Edition, 2017.
© Copyright. Dr. Edward Schellhammer.
All rights reserved.

ISBN-13: 978-1975858407
ISBN-10: 1975858409

www.EdwardSchellhammer.com
www.SchellhammerBusinessSchool.com
www.SchellhammerInstitute.com
www.SchellhammerRetreat.com

TABLE OF CONTENTS

INTRODUCTION

Anything you don't know does not exist for you. As you don't see the processes of destruction of the ecosystems and the species, this threat does not exist for you. You don't see the melting glaciers, the 1-2 cm increase of sea level per year. Therefore, this immense danger for humanity does not exist for you.

You don't see that 75% of the greenhouse gases in the atmosphere will still be there in half a millennium. You don't see the acidification of the oceans with all its effects. You don't see the all-covering contamination with all its horrifying consequences.

You recognize how much you are being brainwashed every day. You don't see the creeping extinction of all human values. You don't see that you are already highly dehumanized. You don't see the dire suffering of 80% of the world population.

You don't see the real worlds behind politics, economy, public education and religion with all their lies and fabrications. Anything you don't know does not exist for you.

Let us be honest, most people are braggers and extremely lazy-minded, and so if this is not enough, we all know that stupidity can't recognize itself.

You reject knowing because the reality would be a frightening shock. But you must open your eyes. You need to know. You must learn. You need to change if you want a humane future.

So, let's explore the core of the human truth:

GENES AND ENVIRONMENTAL INFLUENCES

The genuine code of human development is based biologically and genetically on the polarity of male and female; concrete: penis and vagina; boy and girl (man and woman).

To add: the female body develops breasts that are biologically and genetically a female characteristic and never a male characteristic.

<u>Another genuine code of human development is:</u> penis, vagina and female breast include an energetic lust-factor from zero to a maximum. The lust factor operates naturally and can be stimulated with touching, rubbing, intercourse, sexual images and fantasies, chemical substances, and so on.

The interest in watching and touching the genitals of the other sex (and body) is naturally given and contrary to distorted religious indoctrination it is nothing 'bad'. Intercourse is also a natural drive and creates increasing lust up to orgasm. Increasing lust can also be 'self' produced, which is nothing 'bad'. With the orgasm, the libido (lust) loads falls to (near) zero.

Men and women experience this energetic lust-dynamic with a certain male-female difference in its emotional, mental and behavioral patterns. Sexual experience between man and woman gets a 'spiritual' value (Ying-Yang polarity; anima-animus polarity) if genuine love is the innermost part of sexual activity.

Another genuine code of human development is responsible for mental development. Part of the brain consists of unities responsible for bodily functions. The other part of the brain consists of unities responsible for the mental functions.

A mental function is like a chip, coded for a specific operation such as learning, shaping and training. All males and females have these chips, and as such, whereas a woman has genetically some predominant female shaping characteristics, a man has predominant some male shaping characteristics.

Psychoanalysis also teaches us that during the prenatal phase human beings already begin to develop unconscious complexes (traumas, conflicts). The more negative prenatal experiences about the father and mother, the more negative life experiences during the first three years, the more an intensive drive for compensation, for projection and for a 'true' and 'infallible' spiritual, religious or political home that promises salvation (or prosperity) grows.

The science of 'Epigenetics' teaches us that chemical processes inherited from previous generations (their experiences such as war, violence, scarcity, trauma, etc.) influence gene expressions, which can affect biological processes (health). Additionally, genetic defects can result in genital (and other) deformities.

Parental and cultural influences shape a person during the entire life: Ways of living, attitudes, opinions, rules, social behavior patterns, fabricated legends and especially the transmitted rigid mental state from parents, grand-parents, uncles and aunts, sisters and brothers, authorities, 'friends' and people become shaped by the falsified historical and actual 'truth' of the people's mainstream identity during 3-4 generations.

<u>Environmental influences:</u> We must also consider the many influences a human is exposed to today:

General brainwashing and propaganda, mass media, fabricated religion, standardized public education, economy (consumption), daily news about atrocities and wars (never ended since 1945), suppressed collective fear and other traumatic facts such as violence, loss of security, hunger, unemployment, 'fake news', and so on.

<u>Other aspects shape the male and female identity</u> through gender roles and individual characteristics given by specific religious, cultural or social

environment.

<u>Life is essentially programmed, prenatally:</u> Already during the prenatal stage the fetus experiences the quality of the shaped mental functions of the people around. Positive prenatal experiences are crucial for the fetus:

A happy pregnant mother, a positive parental relationship, peace, daily communication with the fetus (also the father), positive and secure environment, creativity, etc.

<u>There are positive emotional factors</u> that influence <u>the first 3-5 years</u> on the development of the mind: Good social interactions, positive emotional experiences, happiness within the family, expressions of love, understanding, honesty, peace, joy of life, fun, learning stimulations, psychically and spiritually healthy parents, etc.

Joy of life between the parents stimulates positively the development of the brain and the mental functions.

Already during this prenatal stage, the roots for religious and spiritual preferences (beliefs) are established in the brain. Also, the roots for ways of living are established in the brain and the development of mental functions.

Professionally practiced 'regressions' through either meditation or hypnosis, going back up to the prenatal time, have revealed:

A fetus has a soul and this soul (an energetic body) has an extra-sensorial ability to perceive external realities. A fetus can recognize external threats and dangers, good and bad, cheats and scams, truth and lies, falseness and stupidity, love and the character quality of mother and father, the people around, even though the state of the brain (mind) development does not capacitate such perception. Such experiences do however shape the mental functions.

<u>We can therefore conclude:</u> The prenatal experience if fully dependent on archaic, stupid and malformed humans (especially mother and father) will negatively shape the fundamental attitudes towards life and humans.

The prenatal and postnatal experience fully dependent on archaic humans, leads people believing in archaic religions that profess to be 'divine'.

<u>Already prenatally a fetus is exposed to contaminants</u>, toxins, unhealthy nutrition of the mother, external radiation, and so on, with up to 275 toxic elements in the prenatal body that should not be there. Traumatic experiences, mental status of the mother, and environment add to shaping the

mental functions, both before and after birth.

It's self-evident and comprehensible that all these factors can impact on the biological and mental development already during prenatal time and the following 3-5 years.

We can therefore surmise that with 80% of the mental functions shaped and dominated (directly) by a human's mental functions and behavior patterns during his entire life, are then compounded by the build-up of 400 and more toxins in their body, which impair mental functions, the behavior patterns and the shaping process of the self-identity – the result will always be for the worse.

Toxic Chemicals in the Body of the Fetus and Infant: Around 100,000 chemical products are used in Europe. More than 700 carcinogenic elements are present everywhere in the environment in everyday life.

- Tiny doses of chemical residues can have a dramatic effect on the developing fetus.

- Levels of mercury can harm the developing fetal brain.

- Tiny amounts of dioxins and PCBs can damage the developing immune and nervous systems.

- Pollutants and heavy metals cross the placenta, and some also enter the baby via breast milk.

- Chemicals accumulate in different parts of the body including the brain, bones, blood, liver, placenta, etc.

<u>Chemical products can be found</u> in food, water, soil, air, furniture, electrical devices, computers, carpets, cars, paintings and clothes.

Heavy metals in high concentration can also be found in animal bowels, fish and seafood. Poisonous substances can be found in food, in the soil, in the air, in the sea, and then in the body of humans.

<u>Healthy animals are fed with antibiotics every day</u>; it

makes them grow bigger and faster. People who eat meat are getting sicker and sick people are taking longer to recover.

Another example: the sewage that goes into the sea is full of traces of medicines. Fish absorb these, so when eating fish, we take in these chemical elements into our bodies.

Feminized Fishes: Chemicals that flush down the toilet feminize wild fishes; reduce sperm quality, decrease natural aggressive and competitive behavior.

More than 200 chemicals have been found in river water which had characteristics similar to estrogen and antidepressants. Endocrine disruptors, chemicals in pesticides, detergents, antidepressant drugs, contraceptive pill and cosmetics are responsible for change in sex and behavior of fish.

A cocktail of chemical elements (pesticides, neurotoxins, insecticides, etc.) has already killed more than 40% of the species.

Reduced male fertility: The most recent scientific findings indicate that sperm count has reduced in males living primarily in the western world by as much as 52-60%.

Scientists also observed a speedier decline in average testosterone levels in men over the past 30 years. The reasons for both declines are given as environmental!

Gender-bending effects in species: Feminization of the males of numerous vertebrate species is widespread. Fish have been badly hit by man-made gender-bending chemicals.

Wildlife has been found to be contaminated with more than 400 different chemicals.

Results are: Abnormal testes, smaller penises, genital abnormalities and reproductive failures, penises and vaginas, abnormal sperm, hermaphrodites.

Affected species are: Polar bears, whales, falcons, eagles, fishes, high-flying falcons and eagles, bony fish, amphibians, reptiles, birds and mammals, alligators, turtles, frogs, Male herring gulls, starlings, otters, and many more.

A cocktail of chemicals is feminizing males of every class of animals, from fish to mammals, <u>including humans</u>.

<u>Chemicals alter gender:</u> Pregnant women contain greater amounts of the chemicals thus release bigger amounts of it with every excretion. The source of gender-altering pollutants is due to man-made chemicals that are being released globally.

These chemicals have an effect on the sex of many

humans. Chemicals mimic human hormones and trigger changes in the sex-determining process of unborn children. This hormonal influence on the sex-determining process has led to a decrease in the male/female ratio.

Other effects that influence the sex of an individual: a 52-60% decrease in number and quality of sperm and increased deficiency. In respect to the deficiency of the male's reproductive system, these chemicals begin to affect a male already before birth.

Certain chemicals and pharmaceutical substances can influence genital development. Surgical intervention can change a penis into a vagina; and a vagina can be reconstructed into a (small) penis by enlarging the clitoris.

But genetically, the given sex can't be changed!

THE TRANSGENDER SCAM

Simply put, the female sex can't be changed into male and the male sex can't be changed into a female. Surgical, chemical, pharmaceutical or psychological interventions never changes the genuine sex identity determined by the genes.

- Genes are basically the instruction book, while epi-marks direct *how* those instructions get carried out. For example, they can determine when, where, and how much of a gene gets expressed.

- Epigenetic effects might lead to homosexuality when they are passed on from father to daughter or from mother to son.

- Specifically, inherited marks that influence a fetus' sensitivity to testosterone in the womb might 'masculinize' the brains of girls and 'feminize' those of boys, leading to same-sex attraction.

- Sexual orientation can be decided through epi-marks, which are temporary switches in a fetus' DNA that exist while in the womb and shortly after birth.

Scientists confirm there is no Gay gene. The DNA behind sex identity constructions can never change: a male remains a male; and a female remains a female; even with surgical or chemical genital conversion.

Therefore, there is no gene that is responsible for transgender, gay, lesbians, or other sexual and identity orientations.

Genes are responsible for 'normal' biological construction. Gender identity disorders are a neurosis, a mental dysfunction due to environmental, psychological, social, emotional, religious, and now toxic environmental influences; most probably these disorders are already shaped before birth and during the first 3 years of life.

<u>We estimate: the 22 mental functions of 6 billion or more people</u> are already massively and irreparably stunted, damaged, perverted or destroyed.

The sick, neurotic, perverse, decadent, false, mendacious and simply stupid sex identity transgender game has become the 'normal' and 'healthy' status that already some governments protect with laws in order to not 'offend' these (damaged, contaminated, neurotic) individuals.

<u>Transgender claim that their soul is in the wrong body.</u> How do they know that their 'soul' is male or female? Or are all souls sexually multi-faced?

Transgender disorder is simply an obsession. However, the new law protects them. All those who do not accept this will be punished as it is considered 'hate speech' and an offense.

Look at it, this way: Isn't it a serious offense to destroy the healthy, genuine and archetypal concept of male-female? Then again lies have become the truth!

<u>Babies and children are at extreme risk</u> from a cocktail of gender-bending chemicals: waterproof clothes, rubber boots, bed linen, food, nappies, sunscreen lotion and moisturizing cream, etc.

<u>Prominent chemicals are:</u> dioxins, PVC, flame retardants, phthalates (extensively used to soften plastics), dioxins, PCBs and biphenyl-A, all of which mimic the action of estrogen in the body.

Research has documented a connection between prenatal phthalate exposure and 'feminization' of male genitals, including smaller penises.

In other words: Chemicals that should not be in the body are responsible for the transgender issue.

Chemicals that babies are most vulnerable to are in the womb. Hazardous chemicals everywhere are a danger to the health of mind and body.

Transgendered men do not become women. Transgendered women do not become men. Adolescents are "trying out" being transgender to stand out or gain attention from their peers.

Any kind of identity is now regulated by law and some banks have already taken consequences:

People who do not identify as a Mr, Mrs, Miss or Ms will be able to choose from a range of options; gender neutral titles are: Mre, Msr (a combination of Miss and Sir) and Ind, short for individual. Other options include M, Myr, Mx, Sai and Ser. Misc, which stands for miscellaneous, and Pr, an abbreviation for person.

Some universities are already advising students and

staff not to use 'gender-offensive' terms. Previously normal words such as 'he' or 'she' are now gender-offensive if used to describe people that could be either male or female.

Guidance offered by the students' union advises against using traditional pronouns, arguing that doing so suggests there are only two genders. These Universities have threatened to deduct marks from students for using 'gender-offensive' phrases.

Deliberately using the wrong pronoun for a transgendered person is an offence under the union's code of conduct.

Terms such as 'mankind', 'manpower' and 'manmade' are frowned upon by academics if used in essays.

Canada passed a law recently making it illegal to use the wrong gender pronouns. Canadians who do not subscribe to progressive gender theory could be accused of hate crimes, jailed, and fined.

<u>A neurotic gender ideology</u> (which is not a theory) is now put into law by neurotic minds. Whilst the healthy, divine and eternally valid Archetypes are discarded with accusations of hate crimes, fines and jail time.

<u>Nowadays, even Banks offer more 'gender neutral' titles to make 'transgender people feel well.</u> But nevertheless, there are only two sexes – Male and Female! All other forms of gender identities are (usually) distorted mental constructs.

<u>The new 'fake archetype': same sex marriage.</u> Nowadays also: a feminized man <u>marries</u> a masculinized woman. Such types of homosexual marriage are a perversion and elimination of the genuine Archetype called 'marriage' (between a man and a woman).

These initiatives aim to destroy all eternally valid archetypes - boy, girl, man, woman, and family; true love and inner archetypal fulfillment.

Homosexuals and transgender have stolen the eternally valid Archetype of 'marriage'.

There are genetic male and genetic female; versus neurotic sex (identity) reconstructions and chemically produced (contaminants) transgender constructions!

Genetic defects are something very different from the transgender 'constructions' thus we do not enter here into this medical and health issue.

<u>The 'progressive gender theory' is a scam!</u> This scam may bring billions in profits to the pharmaceutical industry and private hospitals with costs for the transgender during their entire life at up to $100,000 and more.

SYSTEMIC DEHUMANIZATION

Since 30 years we observe a fast-increasing collective decadence, an increasing destruction of genuine human values and a collective stultification and dehumanization, which is destroying all the cultural and humane achievements from the past 150 or more years (e.g. Western World).

We can identify the total destruction of all genuine Archetypes of 'the human being' and 'human development'.

Both destructive tendencies go along with the complete destruction of all ecosystems, of humanity as a whole.

Who are the hidden puppet masters? What are their motives? Who benefits from it?

It's all about killing God (= Deicide). But nobody can

kill God; therefore, it's about killing the planet and humanity with an aim to hurt God. The roots are religious and more than 3,000 years old.

The world is facing its all-encompassing and irreversible destruction within 10 years or so.

The 10 biggest threats are all in a complex interrelation and with a momentum that will lead to the point of no return. Nothing can be stopped 'just like that'.

Humanity has reached the point of no return: Humanity has 3 years left to implement global changes of renewal and to rebuild the world within 25 years rooted in the genuine (divine) Archetypes of the Soul.

Since 1988, I have periodically warned authorities and millions of individuals and institutions around the globe about all destructive and suicidal collective developments. Nobody has answered.

Billions of humans pray to their God, and all the prophets from history, to Jesus, 'holy' Mary, and Mohamed, or to other 'holy' men and women.

Today, the NEW PROPHET is on earth, has documented all his inner archetypal processes that are proof of his divine mission and nobody want to examine it and to learn from it.

This shame will lead to the complete elimination of humanity!
Brainwashed! Dehumanized! Cowards! Narcissists! False people! Inflated egomaniacs! Conceited! Pretenders! Hypocrites! Greedy, lazy and lazy-minded!

Too many people don't want to know!

Nevertheless, this has to be understood in the

context that each human is shaped already before birth and during the first 3 years and is the result of poor education, bad environment, false religions, deceitful political system, rampant consumerism, and a mendacious mass media.

Fact is: the systems are impregnable, all-mighty. There is no chance for any breakthrough by individuals for a better society and world.

<u>Genuine human values have to be determined using the following key words:</u>

Human being, life, love, joy, zest for life, lust, full of life, satisfaction, happiness, hope, justice, peace, power of the inner Spirit, centered in the inner Spirit, all-embracing life, totality, completeness, balance, openness, light, confidence, aim, psychical-spiritual evolution, fulfillment, conjunction of the real and spiritual world, fulfillment of the Archetypes of the Soul, source of life, catharsis, renewal, reconciliation, forgiveness, salvation, redemption, and presence of God!

<u>92% of the planet is contaminated. 65% of the ecosystems are irreversibly damaged.</u>

There are a mere 8% of all the genuine human values in the collective life.

It seems most people need the total collapse, mega-wars, absolute poverty, hunger, famine, dire suffering, and cholera included.

Patterns of living and culture are inherited, including traumas from previous generations. History repeats itself until the 'complexes' are identified, changed and renewed by living within the path of the Archetypes of the Soul.

The state of humanity, the world and the planet with all its unstoppable momentum is proof enough of the total failure, the total delusions and aberrations of billions of people with their 'fabricated archaic religion', and the too many highly incompetent politicians and leaders in fundamental systems of society.

The global mess is an expression of the behavior of people, the formed mind of people, the public education, and of all the business schools, the schools of economics and the social sciences.

People get from their leaders what they deserve; and the people never get from their leaders and their religion the truth and what they need in order to live on the path of their inner archetypal development!

Global contamination with all its related destructive effects on the ecosystems and on humans is the primordial threat to humanity caused by the increase of the world population, which will reach 10bn people around 2050 and 12bn people at the end of this century.

The unfolding global drama will be unspeakable horror.

<u>Find a new view about yourself and everything you have in your mind:</u>

- If a European would have been born in Siberia, this person would be a Russian.
- If an American president would have been born in Turkey, he would be a Muslim leader.
- If a German man would have been born in Brazil, he would be all-round Brazilian.
- If a Catholic woman would have been born in a protestant area, she would be a protestant with a protestant Bible.
- If an African man would have been born in Switzerland, he would be Swiss with full Swiss culture.

- If a British politician would have been born in Nigeria, he would be a Nigerian politician and probably a Muslim.
- If a Swede would have been born in Iran, he / she would be an Iranian shaped with the Iranian culture.
- If a Saudi would have been born in a slum in Mexico, he would be a Mexican with all the environmental misery of a slum.

Therefore, all humans are shaped from their culture and environment with all its possible conditions of living. And the souls could not choose the place before they came to earth. Starting with this humanity can find peace.

Most people know nothing that has value. People don't want to know but pretend to know. Their narcissism and greed is disgusting; their boosted ego eats away all human values and great inner potentials.

You must know. You must learn. You must change if you want a humane future. Not wanting to know, to learn, to genuinely lifelong develop, to change and to renew is a shame and a useless being that deserves nothing better than the hell on earth and a dark place in the other world, for 200,000 years far away from God and his light. With all my spiritual and divine power, I order you: "Act now!"

Since 1973 I have been studying and analyzing the global developments and criticalities in politics, economics and economy, wars, public education, psychology, psychoanalysis, archetypal development and religions.

I have explored, analyzed, elaborated and contemplated 100,000 information sources. I have drafted a concept and strategy for global solutions, for changes and renewal. 15,000 dreams have shown me the global mess and the bleak future of humanity, and 3,000 dreams, the (lost) divine archetypal development of humanity and the 'mystery of God'. Most of all findings are elaborated in my books.

FUNDAMENTAL AIMS OF LIFE

- To understand ourselves, our inner life, and behavior.
- To live with a positive life philosophy with real hope.
- To see through, think profoundly, use creativity.
- To become fully self-realized and a strong person.
- To have real, efficient, constructive (practicable) ideals
- To live balanced (meaningful) values, norms, and rules.
- To live with a genuine meaning of life, rooted inside.
- To promote lifelong an authentic holistic growth.
- To live the inner processes for complete fulfillment.

- How do we argue that these aims are fundamental?

- To understand our feelings and to be able to manage them.

- To live love, our genuine psychical needs, with truthfulness.

- To acquire knowledge and skills to efficiently master life.

- To live an authentic life style with efficient self-management.

- To prepare ourselves for a happy relationship and family life.

- To live desire for the other gender, for sex, for love and trust.

- To live free from unconscious biographical burdens.

- To be able to solve difficulties, crises, problems, conflicts.

- To understand the messages from our dreams.

- To care for health, humans, environment, and the planet.

There are billions of humans shaped in billions of ways. We can't determine the 'human' without the mind. Determining the 'Human' leads to the meaning of human's life and human's personal development.

Philosophy: 2400 years of human values

Morality, goodness, ethical principles, prudence, justice, fortitude, faith, hope, charity, beauty of the soul, wisdom, maturity, honesty, braveness, sober-mindedness, harmony of the soul, felicitousness, balanced inner center, humility, peace, inner freedom, discipline, fidelity, self-control, faithfulness, self-knowledge as condition to approach God,
true happiness, love, hope, contemplation, self-reflection, knowledge, self-awareness, will, self-liberation, inner Spirit...

→ Humanity has lost most of these philosophical values!

→ Why does humanity - we all - need such values?

Psychology: 160 years of human values

Self-knowledge, psycho-catharsis, spirituality, unconscious, mind, knowledge about power and inferiority, understanding the mind, the phases of development, love, self-being, understanding needs, understanding behavior and society, humanism, the self-ideal, inner meaning of life, Spirit, meditation, contemplation, balance intellect-emotion or spirituality, learning…

Education: 400 years of human values

Need for learning, ability to learn, morality, the truth, freedom, emancipation, genuine self-realization, authenticity, self-development, shaping character, the higher meaning of life, fulfillment of the genuine (inner) being, love and truthfulness, forming the psychical functions, virtues, will, meaning of life phases, interdependences between humans, realization of meaning, lifelong learning and self-forming, all-embracing education...

The four Fundamental Interest-Dimensions

1) Interest to know: Curiosity, drive to understand, tendency to dedication, thirst to know, need to integrate, consciousness about our creation, love for life, experiences, having an overview.

2) Interest to act: Drive to create, to act, to form, to use, to care, to manage, to educate, to realize plans, to develop, to live consciously, to live culture.

3) Interest in being happy: Lust, pleasure, joy, love, hope, satisfaction, wisdom, wellness, fulfillment, self-realization of all potentials.

4) Interest in becoming a human: Personality education (forming personality) and Individuation as the inner process of growth within the psychical and spiritual dimension (evolution).

What happens with humans if we ignore these interests?

Something is wrong here:

■ Humans explore the planet, biology, material, nano-worlds, and universe; but have a primitive understanding about humans and in particular about themselves.

■ Sciences explore the mind and behavior in order to enslave, brainwash, manipulate, and exploit humans; but never to find the genuine meaning of life.

Modern concepts of spirituality, sects, and religions ignore or abuse the advanced knowledge about humans; in particular they don't promote holistic human evolution.

■ Public education, politics, economics and religion

have a very archaic understanding of humans.

Up to 90% of the world population is mentally malformed. These 90% of humanity have never a chance to get out themselves of this miserable, inefficient, and archaic state of the mind.

■ The leaders around the globe in all economic systems, in politics and governments, in public education, in the mass media, and in religion are themselves imprisoned in their own malformed, distorted, brainwashed, imbalanced and underdeveloped network of their mental functions.

EVERYTHING STARTS BEFORE BIRTH

■ The prenatal time can already be an absolute trauma for a soul that realizes the unconscious archaic ways of living, the archaic characteristics of mother and father and the highly undeveloped people in the environment.

■ The roots of stupidity, greed, falseness, lies, cheat, deceit, arrogance, ignorance, narcissism, blindness, narrow-mindedness, amorality, neuroticism, psychopathy, mental disorder, and so on, become a new interpretation.

■ Malformed and distorted mental functions, behavior disorder, and moral character traits are an expression of a disintegrated (split) human.

■ Critical mental functions, behavior and character are an expression of the separation of the four human dimensions: soul, mind, transcendence (the other world), and terrestrial life.

■ The immanent dynamic of archaic and split state of the collective, the 7.6 billion people (2017), leads to the elimination of human evolution and the destruction of the creation.

COLLECTIVE SELF-KNOWLEDGE

<u>Most people:</u>

- Know themselves on a level of 1-3-5%
- Don't think about their tomorrow
- Don't think about their ways of living
- Believe that they are right with their thinking and judging
- Have no idea about their unconscious inner world
- Believe it is enough what they have learnt
- Can't distinguish between appearances and realities.
- Don't want to learn for love, Spirit, joy, happiness, peace
- Want to be cheated spiritually, religiously, ideologically, economically, politically, educationally, esoterically
- Don't have the necessary knowledge and skills for building up a good life and their fulfillment

Personal Benefit of Self-Knowledge

■ Forms qualification for personal and professional life.

■ Establishes competences for relationships and life.

■ Reduces life risks and suffering over the life course.

■ Creates inner security and trust in one's own forces.

■ Forms an all-sided balanced person (personality).

■ Is indispensable to find enrichment and fulfillment.

■ Reaches the innermost being (the "true Self").

■ Answers the decisive spiritual questions.

Superior Benefit of Self-Knowledge

■ Is applicable everywhere, gives foundation, stabilizes identity.

■ Includes knowledge about humans, life, acting, environment.

■ Qualifies for the right use of leisure, lifetime and

potentials.

- Integrates responsibility for oneself, others, work, society, world.

- Founds the future, in the context of the problems of humanity.

- Is indispensable for education, politics, economics, religion.

- Is indispensable in the future for professional activities.

<u>Importance of Self-Knowledge</u>

- Lack of self-knowledge or low self-knowledge has critical consequences.

- 7.6 billion people (2017) lacking self-knowledge leads humanity towards the abyss.

- The development of a human without self-knowledge creates disasters.

- There is never genuine happiness and fulfillment without profound self-knowledge.

- A relationship between man and woman without

self-knowledge creates uglification.

■ Lack of self-knowledge is essential part of stupidity, arrogance, mental disorder.

→ Self-knowledge is the supreme call for all humans to be and to become a genuine human.

The Human Creation

■ It is a unique gift to be a human, to be on earth, to make a living, and to grow lifelong.

■ Humans go through very different and unique life periods starting as an embryo.

■ The kinds of development are innumerable: biological, psychical (mental), spiritual, behavioral.

■ The manifoldness of experiences humans can make during their life on earth is amazing.

■ Positive and negative life experiences shape and determine the development of human beings.

■ The existence of human beings on earth is not due to a merit; it is a result of the capacity of nature.

STANDARD ATTITUDES OF HUMANS

<u>Critical attitudes are:</u>

- Negation of the psychical life as the fundamental, true, important life
- Rejection of the inner Spirit, the educational power of the dreams
- Restricted by inner (suppressed) conflicts and complexes
- Living without inner experiences (dreams, meditation, introspection)
- No holistic growth; exterior-oriented (forced) development
- Little conscious forming of the mind; predominantly rational areas
- Defense and suppression of uncomfortable facts as much as possible
- Living unconsciously, without being aware of the true inner life

- Tendency to project, identify, and displace (distort) realities

- Establishing life in ideologies, dogmas as a rescuing conception

- Fixing on material objects, on pleasure and fun, on external values

- Undifferentiated experiencing of love, predominantly as egoism

- Giving performances sick values: the best, biggest, superlative

Positive Human Characteristics

- Unity: totality, to be unique, simplicity, organization, structure

- Completeness: necessity, correctness, inevitability, suitability, justice

- Fulfillment; accomplishment: to bring to an end, finiteness, destiny

- Justice: fairness, orderliness, legality, balance

- Process: liveliness, spontaneity, self-regulation,

complete functioning

■ Manifoldness: differentiation, complexity, complicatedness

■ Simplicity: honesty, nakedness, essence, abstract structure

■ Beauty: accuracy, form, vivacity, richness, uniqueness

■ Benevolence: correctness, justice, honesty, understanding

■ Uniqueness: individuality, incomparableness, newness

■ Effortlessness: without forced effort or striving, grace, charm

■ Playfulness: fun, joy, entertainment, festiveness, humor

■ Truth: honesty, nakedness, genuineness, beauty, authenticity

■ Autonomy: self-sufficiency, independency, individuality

■ Creativity: creation, imagination, expression

EVOLUTIONARY HUMAN BEING

<u>The essential characteristics of an 'evolutionary human being' are:</u>

● Accepting psychical life and a conscious forming of all mental forces

● Liberation from inner burdens (biography), free from projecting

● Elaborated images in the unconscious constructively promote life

● Inner orientation: dream interpretation, imagination, contemplation

● Elaboration of all the uncomfortable, weak and different 'things' in life

● Creating relationships, politics, economy, etc., rooted in Individuation

● Dealing with nature, world of animals, and environment with respect

● Differentiated development and use of the power of love and the Spirit

● High flexibility and inner freedom towards material goods and values

● Psychical-spiritual performances with love have highest values

HISTORIC CHALLENGE OF MANKIND

■ There is never a new life without a new holistic understanding of human's mind.

■ There is never a new life without a new holistic public education.

■ There is never a new life without a new holistic governance (politics).

■ There is never a new life without a new holistic balance in the economy.

■ There is never a new life without a new holistic religion (spirituality), rooted in the Archetypes.

■ There is never a new life without new authentic ways of living.

Now, let's explore the human development:

PRENATAL

There are environmental factors that already influence prenatal the development of the <u>brain</u> in a critical way:

Contamination, pollution, dirty water, ignored hygiene, chemicals in food and products, alcohol, tobacco, drugs, certain medicine, lack of basic nutrients (mother), uncomfortable noise, etc.

There are negative emotional factors that influence prenatal the development of the <u>brain </u>in a critical way:

Mother's rejection of the fetus, absence of communication with the unborn, mother's fear or depression, preoccupations, lack of basic nutrients (mother), absence of peace and joy of life, no caring about the fetus, serious fights between parents, fearful environment, stupidity, falseness, life lies of the parents, etc.

There are positive emotional factors that influence the prenatal development of the <u>brain</u>:

A happy pregnant mother, a positive parental relationship, peace, a lot of communication, positive and secure environmental conditions, financial stability, creativity, talking to the fetus (also the father), understanding, etc.

Joy of life between the parents and the child stimulate positively the development of the brain (fetus).

POSTNATAL

There are emotional factors that influence the first 3-5 years the development of the <u>mind</u> in a critical way:

Physical and emotional (verbal) punishments, humiliations, fights between parents, lack of care and communication, no learning stimulations, lack of love, educational rigidity, uneducated parents, exaggerated norms and rules, inappropriate answering to the child's needs for attention and responses to the child's questions, etc.

There are positive emotional factors that influence the first 3-5 years of the development of the <u>mind</u>:

Good social interactions, positive emotional experiences, rich mind of the parents, happiness within the family, expressions of love, understanding between people, honesty and transparency, peace, music of all kinds, joy of life, fun, learning stimulations, psychically and spiritually healthy parents, etc.

During the ages of 2-3 years learning stimulations become fundamental for the mental development:

☺ Communication also with friends

☺ Treating the child sensitively

☺ Reading to the child (tales)

☺ Talking and listening to the child

☺ Interest in the child's emotions

☺ Sensitive age appropriate responses

☺ Being truthful, reasonable, fair

☺ Being reliable in all matters

☺ Answer demand for playing

☺ Being supportive, caring, etc.

MENTAL FUNCTIONS

These are like chips. Each chip has a specific capacity that must be shaped and trained.

The shaping of these chips should correspond to the correct chip code but can be distorted, perverted or ignored.

Only spiritual intelligence cannot be distorted

The Mind consists of mental functions:

1. The manifold operations of thinking

2. Identifying and valuing meaning

3. Experiencing & understanding emotions

4. Forming ideals, attitudes, norms, faith

5. Reservoir of experiences (unconscious)

6. Spiritual intelligence (dreams)

7. Visualization: Meditation, contemplation

8. A multitude of learning capacities

9. Defense and integration mechanisms

10. Problem solving, dealing with criticalities

11. The many kinds of perceptions

12. Identifying and dealing with 'inner needs'

13. Practical intelligence and artistic talents

14. Coded conscience structure

15. Dynamics of psychical energy

16. Unconscious projection dynamics

17. Ability to love and to receive love

18. The energy of the libido, pleasure, drive

19. Inner gender polarity (Animus-Anima)

20. The management functions of the "I"

21. Will and decision making

22. Building up knowledge (information)

Mental functions can be ignored, distorted, stunted, abused, manipulated, etc.

Critical mental functions reduce capacities of making a living, etc.

Critical mental functions create many criticalities in personal life, in relationship life, in love and sex matters, in family life, etc. People create their own inner (mental) prison.

The more the brain is damaged (toxins) and the mental functions malformed or stunted, the less people can become aware of their own poor mental situation.

All mental functions are also essentially shaped and

formed by the conditions of personal environment, biography and society in general

DIGNIFIED HUMAN

A dignified life and human evolution is only possible with basic satisfaction:

Mental Needs:

Learning, evolving, meaning, stimulations, training, forming, identity, individuality, support, nurturing all mental functions corresponding to respective codes
Body Needs:

Protection, nutrition, care, quality, training, wellbeing, relaxation, healthy water and environment, balance

Absence of mental and body needs satisfaction can have lifelong consequences, physically and mentally (emotionally).

Needs for Life:

Efficiency, quality, a home, opportunities, work access to tools, health care, information, education, money, goods, products, social ties, leisure, community, socializing, privacy protection, spirituality.

Needs for Life Perspective:

Hope, peace, justice, fairness, security, learning, honesty, genuine human values, truth, social security, healthy planet, reliable politics, economy, mass media for the truth and for critical thinking Absence of satisfaction for life and opportunities for life perspective can have lifelong consequences, physically and mentally (emotionally).

All mental functions are interrelated, influence each

other and require multiple balances. All functions influence and determine the patterns of behavior and each single kind of behavior.

Behavior and its effects are an expression of the quality and efficiency of the shaped mental functions.

A malformed mind makes life very difficult:

The mind develops through manifold learning processes:

<u>No learning = no development = archaic human being</u>

CONSCIOUSNESS

Input external information:

<u>Consciously or unconsciously selected and partial</u>

Input second hand information: Externally elaborated information such as: Newspaper, Television, Radio, Internet, Books, Magazines, Marketing, Politics, Religion, Education, Movies, Music, Social Media:

Distorted, Reduced, Fabricated, Trivialized, Exaggerated, lies, Brainwash, Whitewashed, Selected, Simplified, Deviating, Deceptive, Delusional, Displaced, Manipulation, Propaganda

Second Hand Information Accepted as 'THE REALITY'

Due to Infantile Trust, Sheep Behavior, Stupidity, Naivety, Ignorance, Thoughtlessness, Libido Ties, and Ways of Living.

Sources of Internal Information are preponderantly ignored: State of Body, Dreams, Intuition, Memory, Unconscious, Extra-sensorial Experiences, Energy, Emotions, Emotional Pain, Meditation, Empathy,

Mood, Inner Needs, Bio-Clock, etc.

<u>Consciousness – Inner Screen</u>

1) Spontaneous semi-conscious 'like-dislike' reaction; Information becomes tied with emotional energy of approval or denial.

2) Conscious manipulative operations of self-interest;

Disposition of attitudes stimulates emotions, shapes internalized realities.

3) Content becomes unconsciously tied with a complex; gets more emotional energy with that.
Thinking can start: Thinking processes are always based on the reality in the 'inner screen'.

<u>Rational Thinking:</u> Identification, Categorizing, Analytical, Systemic, Calculative, Combining, Extrapolative, Cumulative, Creating, Concluding,

Decision Making

<u>Spiritual Thinking:</u> Critical, Creative, Inspiring, Interpretative, Intuitive, Valuing, Meditative, Meaning-Oriented, Dream-rooted, Faith Building

<u>Instinctive Defense Thinking:</u> Selfish, Lazy, Self-Protecting, Obstinate, Prejudging, Rigid-Normative, Emotional, Libido-Driven, Impulsive, Instinctive, Main-Stream-Opinionated, Blinded, Dogma-Belief, Fixated, Greedy, Envious, Irrational, Aggressive

UNCONSCIOUS COMPLEXES

Psychoanalytical Knowledge:

- All kinds of 'complexes' and habits are shaped prenatal and during early childhood
- If a pregnant mother eats a lot of junk food, the fetus stores this habit and will copy it later
- A habit itself consists of a pattern of connected environmental factors

- Behavioral, eating and cultural habits are transferred over several generations

Already Sigmund Freud, Leopold Szondi, and Carl Gustav Jung (among others) discovered the dynamic of inherited 'complexes' during several generations.

Complexes are patterns of mental disorder: traumas, unsolved problematic mental or behavioral patterns.

Complexes have an intrinsic energy that forces the individual to repeat the destructive patterns unless it is solved.

<u>Factors that influence epigenetic changes prenatal and postnatal:</u>

Famine, (mal-) nutrition, emotions, mother's diet, obesity, depression, anxiety, stress, psychological and physical abuse or neglect but also happiness, stability, a flourishing life environmentally induced including from grand-parents.

Stress on the fetus and infant leads to lifelong health consequences.

For example, famine and malnutrition from the mother result in inherited psychical and mental patterns, affective disorders, obesity, and antisocial personality disorder.

Food preferences and certain behavior pattern are also already prenatal transmitted from the mother to the infant.

Prenatal experiences and during the first 3-5 years decisively shape the mind for the rest of the life.

Meditative regressions up to the prenatal time lead to a new understanding of humans.

Many dire suffering, serious problems and difficulties

in life, and the immense global criticalities have roots in prenatal formation and during early childhood.

- Regressions unveil key principles and processes of human evolution that start during prenatal time.

- Humans are responsible for their development; they have a free will to choose the direction.

- What most people become, are, think, believe, do and live have effects for centuries.

<u>Human's history repeats itself!</u>

MIND SHAPING RESULTS

Blinded, Naïve, Gullible, Lazy, Ignorant, Brainwashed, Seduced, Deformed, Distorted, Disfigured, Stupid, Unreasonable, Stunted, Stubborn, Indifferent, Superficial, Self-alienated, Soulless, Lies, Life-lies,

Falseness, Cheat, Deceit, Predacious, Conceited, Bragger, Impostor, Enslaved, Exploited, Abused, Violated, Neurotic, Perverse, Narcissistic, Psychotic, Psychopathic, Greedy, Ravenous, Religious-psychotically Driven, Sheep, Obsessed, Ideological Fanatics, Insatiable, Brutal, Ego-driven, 'I do what I want'-Ego, Follower, Copycat, Coward, Hypocritical, Aggressive, Suppressing, Displacing, Distorting, Exploiting, Stealing, Destroying, Enslaving, Desecrating, Oppressing, Breaker, Killer, Embitterer, Bellicose, Destroyer of Nature and Ecosystems, Murder of the Truth and Genuine Human Values ...

Fact: The state of the mind dictates the behavior with all consequences, individually and collectively.

ARCHETYPAL HUMAN EVOLUTION

Personal Development

Meditative Regressions say: From the moment of

conception and during the prenatal time, a fetus has:

- Extra-sensorial perception

- Self-awareness (identity)

- Emotional experiences

- An idea about meaning

- A sense for human values

80% of mental functions are shaped prenatal and postnatal during the first 3-5 years.

Archetypal human evolution is based on the right way of shaping. With archetypal (genuine) personal development an adult can reshape and develop his mental functions up to optimal efficiency and balance.

This is 'INDIVIDUATION'

The process includes:

Love and Skills for Life; Zest and Skills for Work; Self-Management Skills; Meaningful Self-Realization; Realization of Potentials; Happiness, Joy of Life; Holistic Fulfillment; Growing for Completeness; Interest in Knowledge; Truth and Truthfulness.

In the collective unconscious, there is something like an 'oath' which 'obliges' all human beings to believe:

"The evolutionary, psychical-spiritual human being doesn't exist."

If you want to live an authentic self-realization, then you have to know yourself well and the consequences must lead to concrete actions.

The alternative to Individuation is:

Regression, unconscious being, ignorance, no Spirit, negation of life, reduction of life, self-alienation, archaism, dogmatism, and fundamentalism.

The Schellhammer Archetypal Pyramid

The Development of Human Needs:

Prenatal Needs: Attention, Acceptance, Care, Basic Communication, Healthy Nutriments, Constructive Social Life, Healthy Environment, Responsible and Prepared Parents for the Fetus' Growth, Healthy and Genuine Emotional-mental State of the Mother

Ages 1-3 year Needs: Guidance for Learning Opportunities and Explorations, Evolving Existential Dependence, Healthy Life for Mental and Social Development, Access to Extensive Explorations, Protection, Care and Communication Stimulus

Ages 4-6 year Needs: Basic Knowledge, Extensive Basic Learning, Guidance in Understanding and Managing Emotions, Skills for Daily Life Issues, Strong Parental Communication and Interactions, Mental and Physical Stimuli

Ages 7-12 year Needs: Basic Development of Mental Functions, Self-Discovering, Exploring the near Worlds, Shaping Behavior Patterns, Self-Organization, Adaptation of Rules, Shaping Self-Identity, Creativity

Adolescence 13-18 year Needs: Learning, Knowledge, Higher Development of Mental Functions, Discovering Sexuality, Protection, Exploring Worlds, Becoming Self-Responsible,

Adaptation of Human Values

Young Adult 19-35 year Needs: Forming Self-Realization and Identity, Discovering Life Perspectives, Male-Female Polarity, Learning for Work, Work Opportunities, Learning for Life and Meaning, Lifelong Learning, Reaching High Level of Self-knowledge

Adult Age 36-50 year Needs: Self-Realization reaches its full strength, Well Shaped and Revised Mental Functions, Completeness and Fulfillment form Stream of Professional and Personal Responsibilities

Senior Adult 51-65 year Needs: Significant Level of Wisdom, Maturity, Balanced Personality, Social Responsibility, Extensive Inner Development, High Professional and Ethical Responsibility and Mission for the Collective

Third Age Needs: Understanding the, Genuine

Meaning of Life, of Humans and the World, Archetypal Experiences about the 'Mystery of Human Evolution' to Transmit to the Young Generations, Health Support, Guidance for Development

<u>Basic Need for the Lifespan of ALL Humans:</u>

Healthy Food, Water, Air, Environment, Shelter, Security, Protection, Care, Health Care, Learning, Work, Money for Living, Responsibility, Education, Inner Development, Justice, Peace, Ethics, Hope, Love, Truth, Knowledge, Human Values, Meaning, Sexuality, Genuine Spirituality, Evolving Capacities

Dr. Edward Schellhammer

THE FOUNDER

Dr. Edward Schellhammer is the founder and President of the Schellhammer Education Group that includes the Schellhammer Business School, the Schellhammer Institute and the Schellhammer Retreat.

What is most striking about meeting Dr. Edward Schellhammer beyond his pleasant and polite manner; youthful disposition or passionate and sincere views on humanity and the planet, is his unshakable conviction that the world needs a new pioneering education.

But exactly who is Dr. Edward Schellhammer? Is he a Philosopher, an expert on human matters, a Psychologist, a prolific author of over 30 titles from psychology to politics and economics, an educator, or a visionary with a profound and beneficial insight into the human condition?

The answer is that he is all that and more. In different age, he would have been called a polymath, and probably kept close company with those giants of The Age of Enlightenment, like his fellow countryman Jean Jacques Rousseau, Thomas Payne and perhaps even Thomas Jefferson. For, it is exactly this gift of enlightenment that Dr. Schellhammer wants to give humanity.

He reveals: "My studies, global travels, professional experiences and extensive study and research since 1970 have given me a clear and unique insight into humanity, human evolution, spirituality, education, cultures, needs, values, standards and our purpose in life like no other!"

Pausing to add: "Humanity hasn't even begun to discover what the true path of human life on earth is fundamentally good and right for".

Born and educated in Switzerland he has lived in

Paris, South of France, London, Kiel, Detroit, and Mexico, before settling in Marbella, Spain, some 27 years ago.

He studied Education, Psychology, Psychoanalysis, and Philosophy. He was a lecturer at the University of Zurich as well as other institutions, and as a member of international workshops he dedicated his ample energy to futurology, future perspectives of humanity, peace and disarmament, development of education in Latin America and key global issues in general, concentrating on developing a new understanding of politics and economics for the future. His findings are indispensable for all those who value life, love, and justice.

He places great emphasis on Dream Theory a subject that he has researched for most of his life and passionately believes in, declaring that some 35 years ago he had a dream that told him to solve the mystery of man and human evolution. Stating categorically: "My initial reaction was, this is an impossible task!" and then quickly adds with equal conviction: "But today, I think, no, I know, that I have discovered all the fundamental components that explain the mystery of man and human evolution."

With his professional background, he has written many books spanning: Individuation (holistic personal development), Dream Theory and Interpretation, Problem Solving, The Individual and Collective Unconscious, Love and Relationships, The Archetypes of Man, The Future of Humanity, Global Human Education, New Philosophical Anthropology, Didactics in Teaching and Counseling and Coaching.

All inner processes – psychical, spiritual and practical – to find and live the (archetypal) codes of human evolution are well documented like never before in the history of mankind. Everything that you need to learn is elaborated in his books.

Dr. Edward Schellhammer has unveiled the mystery of mankind, the psychological-spiritual and archetypal codes of human evolution. It has taken 35 years to understand humans, the divine and factual human evolution, the mendacious aims of politics, economy, public education, religion, spirituality, and the state of humanity and the world, in order to offer you today the eternally valid concept (codes) of the Archetypal Human Evolution.

During the last 35 years he had around 14,000 dreams about the state and development of humanity, the world and the planet. Countless dreams have shown him everything of fundamental relevance for humanity's future and evolution.

During the same period, he also had estimated 3,000 dreams about the genuine archetypal evolution of mankind, the state and potentials of the mind and of the world population, the 'other world' and God. He has been in his dreams in the 'other world', in the divine paradise, and he has experienced the 'Union with God' as well as many more archetypal processes. He profoundly elaborated all this; estimated 80,000 hours of explorations and analysis in total.

Dr. Edward Schellhammer says: "The never achieved most advanced psychological, spiritual, archetypal, educational and practical concept, the Philosophical Anthropology of the Archetypal Human Evolution, is prepared and can lead humanity to hope, peace, justice, balance, truthfulness, and fulfillment."

Like the man himself his books are not for the faint hearted with challenging, pioneering and vanguard content and new ways of thinking that covers shaping of the mind, personal development, human values, human evolution, life, business, politics, economy, society, education, and religion – for everybody that is searching for the truth and for a fundamental personal fulfillment. Reading his books is pure adventure for the mind.

After decades of extensive explorations, research, analysis, writing and sometimes personal retreat, Dr. Edward Schellhammer is now at the disposal of discerning individuals and institutions wishing to pursue prepared and tailor-made programs of evolutionary further education.

HUMANITY NEEDS A NEW CONCEPT FOR 'MANKIND', A NEW SPIRITUALITY, AND A NEW BREED OF EVOLUTIONARY HUMANS!

HUMANITY NEEDS A NEW GENERATION OF ALL-ROUND PREPARED LEADERS IN EVERY FIELD OF HUMAN ENDEAVOR!

HUMANITY NEEDS A NEW CONCEPT OF BUSINESS SCHOOLS, OF UNIVERSITIES, AND OF A NEW PUBLIC EDUCATION!

HUMANITY NEEDS TO RECLAIM THE ARCHETYPAL SPIRITUALITY ('RELIGION') THAT WAS NEVER ESTABLISHED IN THE PAST!

17.04.2011 I dreamt: "The door to Paradise must now be completely closed for all souls, until the complete enlightenment of the truth is fulfilled globally." Therefore, with all the power of attorney from my spiritual (archetypal) authority [that has given it to me in dreams] and in order to save the human evolution I decide today:

I will not let a single soul into Paradise, apart from a few exceptions, until the deicide octopus is detected and disclosed, until the truth is researched and clarified and put on the table, and until both are fully understood by the entire humanity. Everyone is summoned to work on this catharsis and renewal: Researchers, experts, scientists, journalists, politicians, legal professionals, CEOs, and all varieties of power holders and religious officials; but also, all and every single citizen of all states and nations.

"As the highest judge of all souls living in the other world and of all souls living today and in the future on this earth, I will severely punish the supreme masters of deicide with a minimum of 50,000 years being far away from God and his light, the protagonists with a minimum of 10,000 years, and all other significant collaborators of deicide will not see God and his light for a very long time. People that are unwilling to learn and to develop themselves psychically and spiritually and those who infect the collective (entire societies) with brainwashing, lies and falseness, with their insane narcissism, perverse neurosis, psychosis, psychopathy and madness cannot expect to be allowed to enter into paradise. It is said since millenniums: If a folk and its government ignore its new (genuine, provable) prophet, destroy his life, bans him, and paralyzes with that his divine mission for humanity and the archetypal human evolution, this folk will lose its land. Switzerland is already sentenced. The same punishment is applied for any folk that acts in the same way against this prophet for humanity in the third Millennium. If all of humanity accepts the deicide simply by ignoring it, then most souls will be sent for 200,000 years to a dark place far away from the paradise of God."

THE FOUNDATION FOR A NEW PATH

THE MANIFESTO (ISBN: 1494855917): The book unveils the state of people, of humanity, of the world and the planet. People destroy the evolution of humanity with their blinded religious, atheist or other mental or political insanity. The Manifesto puts the challenge on the table, as never before! Not wanting to know is a shame. How can you be happy with a suppressed shame? You can only become free inside with knowledge, critical thinking, and self-contemplation. This book tells you the 'truth' about the world and the lost archetypal path of humanity!

ARMAGEDDON OR EVOLUTION (ISBN: 1484868668): There are only two options: Humanity's leaders take responsibility to manage evolution in a sustainable manner, or the systemic fissures will crush mankind and the planet will degenerate. The book reveals how everybody can contribute to a sustainable human life. Why should you have a good life if you don't contribute for a better world? The book contains all you need to know about the species called 'human': fulfilling ways of living, evolutionary personality development, man-woman-relationship aiming for 'completeness', a substantial advanced philosophy about humans, and a realistic overview of the big problems around the globe.

THE FUTURE IN YOUR HANDS (ISBN: 1478377917): The truths and facts are outrageous and beyond all imagination. The damages worldwide are monstrous. Everybody pays with their taxes during centuries for ignoring the ongoing massive destruction and wars. Nevertheless, everybody can contribute to create a new path for humanity. The state of humanity and the world - preprogrammed from previous generations - shows us that most parents don't care about what the future will bring to their children. If parents don't care about the future of their children, then the young generation must learn to take their future into their own hands!

DEICIDE (ISBN: 1478366524): Indicted: The supreme masters of neo-capitalism, the leaders of corporations, banks, politics, media, justice, the ultra-high net worth individuals, the leaders of education, universities, Christianity; humans that destroy the genuine human values and that accept the lies as the truth. Those who seriously want to understand the mess also get the conceptual solutions. A must read for all those who work in the education sector, in politics, economy or religion.

BECOME A STRONG PERSONALITY (ISBN: 1478372958): The book provides everything that all people must develop for a sustainable inner foundation in order to be prepared for a fast-changing world. It is ridiculous and stupid if you do not want to become a genuine, strong personality. Read this to prepare yourself for the world!

LOVE YOUR LIFE (ISBN: 1478372834): Everybody needs to build up the ability to love, and to live joy of life. The book provides everything that must be developed in order to find happiness. Most people do not have the slightest idea what love is about. It's much more than an emotion. A must for anyone interested in genuine love!

60 DAYS TO PARADISE (ISBN: 1480177369): Everybody needs to learn about how to develop a better life. The book provides countless tips and practical suggestions to reach genuine success. The paradise is within you. Therefore: Do you want darkness and the hell inside or the eternal sun? You will find out how to create your inner sun.

PRACTICAL PSYCHOLOGY (ISBN: 147836694X): The book provides immense knowledge about humans, human life and human concerns; countless exercises promote personal development, a better life, and professional competences in matters of human life. 90-95% of all humans are archaic humans like people who lived 1000 and 2000 years ago. It is really urgent that you evolve with this book to a very valuable inner status of quality and being.

PSYCHOLOLGY I (ISBN: 1478370661): This book expands the frame of 'Practical Psychology' and presents more precise knowledge about matters of human life and the mind. A lot of practical exercises allow one to reach a high level of genuine personal development. Read rubbish and live with delusions. Remain ignorant. Or take this book in your hands and start becoming a complete and fulfilled human with a precious soul and efficient mind.

POLITICS (ISBN: 1480198714): Politics has failed in

achieving peace on earth, in eliminating the roots of all wars, in creating economic balance, and in promoting human evolution. Outrageous failure! The world needs 10 million and more new politicians and leaders with all-encompassing advanced knowledge and the right personal development. Before you talk about politics and leadership, read this book!

ECONOMICS I (ISBN: 1478226730): The book unveils the dogma and ideology of the biggest scam in modern history that led to the degradation of humanity and the planet via 'profits at all costs'. All business people and those who work in a field of the economy must know what the academic education does not tell you. If you don't want to know, you are a collaborator of the collective destruction.

ECONOMICS II (ISBN: 1478244577): The book delves into the key elements of microeconomics and their intricate relation to financial crises and the omnipresent destructivity exerted on humanity. This book teaches you what you will not learn in accredited economic teaching. Become a robot and servant of the capitalist cynicism or learn about the lies and scams for a new economic world.

ECONOMICS III (ISBN: 1478275626): The book uncovers key facts and figures of the state of humanity and the planet; revealing herewith the systemic failures in economics, politics, education and religion. Not wanting to know about the roots of failures in the economy, in politics, education and religion serves the hidden masters, which systematically destroy the archetypal (genuine) human development. Therefore: Expand your view and serve the human development!

MODERN DREAM THEORY (ISBN: 1478384891): Dreams guide people to the truth, to the power of the inner Spirit. Dream form the ethical, psychological, spiritual and religious foundation of life. Dream shed light on all the principles of the psychical-spiritual growth. Without the 'Spiritual intelligence' of dreams, people can never find fulfillment. There is no better guidance for everyone, regardless of culture, religion or ideology. There is no future for humanity, without taking the power of the inner Spirit seriously.

200 WAYS TO SAVE THE PLANET (ISBN: 1548039209): "Humanity has 25 years left to implement relevant and all-encompassing changes, but must start now." Herein, Dr. Schellhammer outlines 200 concrete ways of practical change for every human being around the globe that can guarantee a change from the cataclysmic roller coaster ride that humanity finds itself on today to a complete renewal in order to bring humanity "back to the path of (archetypal) genuine human evolution," he says.

All books available worldwide on Amazon, in paperback and Kindle version. For German versions, see schellhammerinstitut.com.

SCHELLHAMMER RETREAT

The Schellhammer Retreat is an educational institution that offers a one-of-a-kind Retreat together with a unique self-development educational program. The Schellhammer Retreat is about discovery, spirituality, fulfillment and self-exploration through the process of Individuation. Participants are offered a breakthrough in their personal life, fulfillment in their vocation, a deeper archetypal meaning of life, an inner catharsis, and the complete absolution.

The Schellhammer Retreat is a psychical-spiritual 'Life School' that can lead individuals to high and very high aims of the Individuation Process. It includes the shaping processes of any kind of mission for humanity and the genuine (archetypal) human evolution.

Book yourself a stay: SchellhammerRetreat.com.

9 781975 858407